Giant Stories

by Stan Cullimore

Contents

PEARSON
Longman

The Giant Who Cried

It was a hot, sunny day.
Karl and Sally went to the park with Dad.

They played on the swings.

"I'm hot," said Karl.
"So am I," said Sally. "Let's play in the pool"

But the pool was empty.
There was no water.

"I'm so hot," said Sally.
"So am I," said Karl.
They sat on the grass under a tree.

6

"Look at that!" said Karl. "It's a giant!"

"Hello," said the giant. "Let's play."
Karl, Sally and Dad ran away.

The giant sat on the grass.
He started to cry. His tears rolled down his
nose.

His tears rolled into the pool.
Soon it was full of water.
"Thank you," said Sally. "Now we can play in
the pool."

So they did!

Wag, Bag, Boo - How Do You Do?

Once upon a time a giant came to the town hall.
"Wag, bag, boo – how do you do?" he said.

The mayor came out of the town hall.
"Wag, bag, boo – how do you do?" said the
giant.
"Help!" shouted the mayor. "A big, horrid giant!"

The mayor ran back into the town hall.
He picked up the telephone.
"Send for the police," he said.

The police came to the town hall.
"Wag, bag, boo – how do you do?" said the
giant.

"Help!" shouted the police. "A big, horrid giant!"
They ran into the town hall.

The mayor picked up the telephone.
"Send me some soldiers," he said.

Some soldiers came to the town hall.
"You are a big, horrid giant. We will soon get rid
of you!" said the soldiers.
The giant looked at the tanks. He was scared.

The giant said, "Wag, bag, boo – how do you do?"

"Wag, bag, day – I'm OK," the little girl said.

The giant smiled.

"See?" the little girl said to the mayor. "He is not a big, horrid giant. He just wants to be friends."

And the little girl took the giant home for tea.

The Giant and Jack

Once upon a time there was a giant who lived
at the top of a beanstalk.
He lived in a lovely giant house with his pet
goose, Milly.
They were very happy and they had lots of fun
together.

One morning the giant said to Milly. "What shall
we do today?"
"I'm going to lay an egg," said Milly.
"Will it be made of gold?" asked the giant.
"Yes," said Milly. "All my eggs are made of
gold."

So Milly laid her golden egg.
"What shall we do with this one?" asked the giant.
"Let's take it to the market and swap it for something nice," said Milly.

So they went to the market and looked around.
"That looks nice. What is it?" asked the giant.
"It's a magic harp that plays lovely music," said
Milly.
So they swapped the golden egg for the magic
harp.

They took the magic harp home.
Then the magic harp played and the giant
danced with Milly.

"I'm tired," said the giant. "I need a rest."

"So do I," said Milly.

They sat down and fell fast asleep.

A boy crept into the giant's house.
His name was Jack.
He had climbed up the beanstalk to see what
was at the top.

Jack picked up the magic harp. "This looks nice!"
Milly woke up. "What are you doing?" she
asked.
"I'm taking this harp and I'm taking you," said
Jack.
He grabbed Milly and ran out of the giant's
house.

"Help," shouted Milly. "A horrid boy is stealing me!"

The giant woke up. "Come back here you thief!" he shouted.

He ran out of the house after Jack.

Jack climbed down the beanstalk.
He was just going to chop it down when the giant arrived.
"You are a thief," said the giant.
He picked up Milly and the magic harp.
Just then, a policeman arrived.

"This thief ran away from prison," said the policeman.

"I have come to take him back."

So Jack went back to prison.

The giant, Milly and the harp went back to the house at the top of the beanstalk.

And they lived happily ever after.